Amazing Animals

Raccoons

Please visit our Web site, www.garethstevens.com. For a free color catalog of all our high-quality books, call toll free 1-800-542-2595 or fax 1-877-542-2596.

Library of Congress Cataloging-in-Publication Data

Baicker, Karen.
    Raccoons / Karen Baicker.
        p. cm. — (Amazing animals)
    Includes index.
    ISBN 978-1-4339-4020-0 (pbk.)
    ISBN 978-1-4339-4021-7 (6 pack)
    ISBN 978-1-4339-4019-4 (library binding)
    1. Raccoon—Juvenile literature. I. Title.
    QL737.C26B352 2011
    599.76'32—dc22
                                                    2010011545

This edition first published in 2011 by
Gareth Stevens Publishing
111 East 14th Street, Suite 349
New York, NY 10003

This edition copyright © 2011 Gareth Stevens Publishing.
Original edition copyright © 2006 by Readers' Digest Young Families.

Editor: Greg Roza
Designer: Christopher Logan

Photo credits: Cover, back cover, pp. 4-5, 8-9, 14-15, 18-19, 20-21, 21 (right), 24-25, 25 (bottom), 28-29, 30-31, 34-35, 37 (bottom), 38-39, 42-43, 44-45, 46 Shutterstock.com; pp. 1, 3 © Digital Vision; pp. 6-7, 10-11 © Corbis; pp. 12-13 © iStockphoto.com/James Ward; pp. 16-17 © Nova Development Corp.; p. 17 (bottom) © iStockphoto.com; p. 18 (bottom) © iStockphoto.com/Craig Veltri; pp. 22-23, 32-33, 36-37 Photodisc/Getty Images; pp. 26-27 © iStockphoto.com/Holger Ehlers.

Printed in the United States of America

CPSIA compliance information: Batch #CS10GS: For further information contact Gareth Stevens, New York, New York at 1-800-542-2595.

Amazing Animals
Raccoons

By Karen Baicker

 **Gareth Stevens**
Publishing

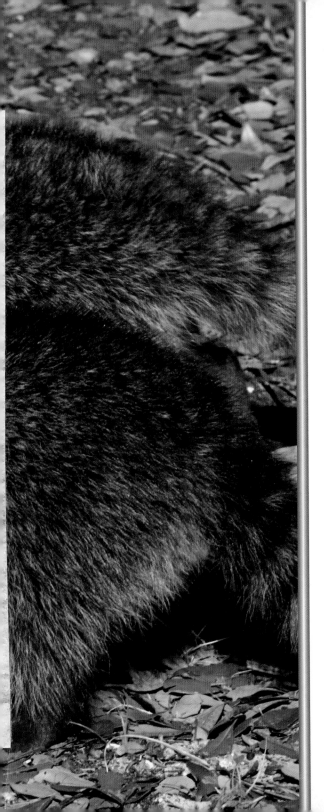

Contents

Chapter 1
A Raccoon Story

Cute Kits!

A baby raccoon is called a kit. Other animal babies are called kits as well. These animals include skunks, rabbits, foxes, and weasels.

It's a sunny afternoon in April, and Mother Raccoon is curled up in her den with four newborn babies. The babies look like tiny balls of fluff. They won't be able to see until they're a few weeks old. They spend their days and nights snuggling with Mother Raccoon and drinking her milk.

During the next few months, Mother Raccoon stays very close to her babies and keeps them safe. She moves them to a new den every other night. She uses her mouth to carry each kit gently by the scruff, or back of its neck, to a new home high in a tree trunk. Up there, the young kits can't be seen by dogs and coyotes. But Mother Raccoon is always watching for owls and eagles.

Soon, the kits are able to walk and climb. They have black fur around their eyes and ringed tails. They look like tiny copies of Mother Raccoon.

Most nights, Mother Raccoon leaves the kits alone for a while as she looks for food. She eats some and brings what she can carry back to the den for the kits. But tonight is extra special. It's time for the kits to leave the den and find their own food.

Mother Raccoon climbs down the tree, and the kits follow in a line. They aren't good climbers like Mother Raccoon is. One of the kits loses his grip and almost falls. But he manages to hang on to a nearby vine—upside down! Mother Raccoon rescues the terrified kit and helps him climb back onto the tree.

Once on the ground, the kits continue to follow their mother in a line. But they're curious about everything they see, hear, and touch. Soon Mother Raccoon hears the sound of high-pitched crying. She glances behind her to see if her kits are okay. One, two, three . . . where is her fourth kit? She follows the crying sound to a big log. The smallest kit is crying because he's lost. She picks him up by his scruff and puts him back into line with the other kits.

The raccoon family reaches a stream. The kits watch as their mother dips her paws into the water. With a splash, she tosses a floppy crayfish to her kits! Yummy! The kits copy their mother and try to catch their own crayfish.

Life Alone

Adult raccoons don't hang around with each other. They like to live alone. But a mother raccoon stays close to her kits until they're fully grown.

Name That Critter!

The word "raccoon" comes from the Native American word *aroughcun*, meaning "he who scratches with his hands."

Suddenly, Mother Raccoon hears a noise in the leaves. It's a fox! Quickly, she pushes her kits toward the closest tree and gives them a shove to help them up the trunk. Then her fierce **instincts** take over. She moves toward the fox with her sharp teeth bared. She shrieks at him and chases him down the stream until he's far away from her young ones. Mother Raccoon returns to her kits. She makes a new den for them in the hollow of a different tree, just in case the fox returns.

From now on, the kits will be leaving their dens more often—and they'll search for food on their own. But they still have much to learn from their mother. They'll have to learn everything before the weather turns cold. By then, they'll be full-grown raccoons. It will be time to leave their mother—and each other—and find their own places to live.

Mothers Rule!

Male raccoons pair up with females to mate. But then they usually leave. Fathers have nothing to do with raising kits. Moms are in charge!

Chapter 2
The Body of a Raccoon

Raccoons are very curious, which helps them survive. Sticking their noses or paws into every hole often rewards them with tasty treats. A well-fed raccoon is more likely to have a long life.

Masked Bandits!

A raccoon is easy to identify by the dark fur that grows around its eyes. It looks like a mask! The mask makes the raccoon look like a bandit. Many farmers who wake up to find their crops eaten by raccoons would agree. So would people who find their garbage cans knocked over!

The raccoon usually has white or light fur above the mask and on both sides of its **snout**. It has long whiskers, and its pointed ears are tipped with white fur. It has 40 teeth, most of which are sharp. The teeth can tear into almost anything the raccoon wants to eat. A raccoon's paws are almost as skillful as human hands. They help a raccoon get into a lot of places, such as a garbage can or even a refrigerator!

A Telltale Tail

A raccoon's tail is as easy to recognize as its mask. The tail is long and bushy, and has five to eight dark rings. When climbing and running, the raccoon holds its tail straight out behind it for balance.

Furry Coats

An adult raccoon weighs between 10 and 20 pounds (4.5 and 9 kg)—about the weight of a small dog. Raccoons in cold climates weigh more than those in warm areas. Males are heavier than females.

A raccoon has two layers of fur. The top layer—made of rough, heavy **guard hairs**—acts like a waterproof raincoat. This layer has light-colored and dark-colored hairs, sometimes with a touch of yellow. The second layer of fur is much softer. In the winter, a raccoon's fur is at its warmest and woolliest. It makes the raccoon look like a little bear.

Fashion Tails!

Unfortunately for raccoons, people have long sought raccoon fur for clothes. Native Americans wore raccoon-skin robes. European settlers used the skins to make jackets and caps. In the 1920s, raccoon-skin coats were a fad for male college students. The biggest craze came in the 1950s with Davy Crockett hats, like the one shown here.

A hollow high in a tree trunk is a raccoon's favorite location for its den.

A raccoon can spread its fingers far apart. This helps the animal do all kinds of things. It can even open a soda bottle and drink from it!

Give Me Five!

The raccoon's five-fingered paws look a lot like human hands. But watch out! Those fingers have sharp claws. The raccoon's paws aren't quite like human hands. Humans have thumbs that can bend to touch their other fingers. Raccoons don't. But they can do many humanlike things with their long, flexible fingers. Raccoons can turn doorknobs, open cabinets, and remove tops from jars!

Going Places

Raccoons walk on all fours just as bears do—with the bottoms of their paws completely flat on the ground. The tracks made by a raccoon look a lot like human handprints.

Raccoons don't move quickly because they're so heavy for their size. But they're excellent swimmers and climbers. A raccoon can turn its hind feet so that they face backwards. This lets it dig its claws firmly into a tree trunk as it climbs down headfirst!

Chapter 3
Creatures of the Night

Raccoons see things that are near very clearly, but they can't see faraway things very well. They don't see colors. Raccoons see everything in shades of gray.

nights Out!

Raccoons are **nocturnal** (nahk-TUHR-nuhl). That means they're active during the night and sleep during the day. Eating at night means there's less competition with other animals for food. When the sun goes down, raccoons leave their dens and go to their favorite feeding spots. In the wild, that might be a stream or pond. In towns and cities, it might be your garbage cans. From night to night, raccoons remember where the good feeding spots are.

night Sight

Like other nocturnal mammals, raccoons have excellent night vision. The **pupils** in their eyes open wide to let in as much light as possible. Special cells deep in their **retinas** act like mirrors and shine all the light back into the eyes. That magnifies even a small amount of light. That's how a raccoon can see so well at night and why its eyes seem to glow in the beam of a flashlight.

Super Senses

Raccoons depend on their excellent hearing to survive. To raccoons, rustling leaves sound like a loud rumble. This helps raccoons make successful getaways from **predators**. This is important because they're not fast runners! Raccoons also have a great sense of smell. They can smell an acorn that's fallen into a pile of leaves and a mouse hiding in the grass. They also use smell to identify food.

The sense of touch is important at night, and raccoons have very sensitive paws. They pick things up and roll them around in their fingers over and over as a way to identify them. Raccoons' whiskers also help them feel things.

A Long Winter's Nap

Raccoons don't **hibernate** all winter like bears do, but they do sleep a lot. They may stay in their dens for several weeks. When the weather is milder, they go outside to search for food. Then they go back to their dens and repeat the process.

Raccoons put on extra weight during the fall. They may not eat for many weeks during winter and must live off the fat they've stored. By the end of winter, they've lost up to half their weight.

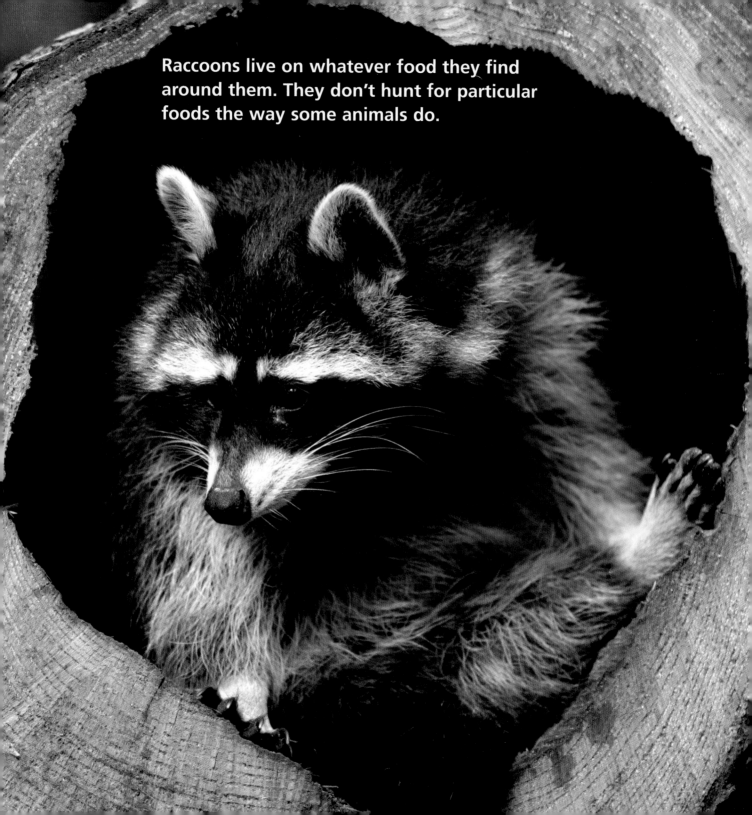

Raccoons live on whatever food they find around them. They don't hunt for particular foods the way some animals do.

Dipping and Dunking

Raccoons often dunk their food into water and rub it between their paws before eating. People once thought they were washing their food. The raccoon's scientific name is *Procyon lotor* (PROH-see-ahn LOH-tuhr). *Lotor* means "washing."

Then scientists noticed that raccoons in zoos wet their food although it wasn't dirty. Raccoons also make a dipping motion with their food even when there's no water to wash it in. Scientists decided that dipping food in water, even imaginary water, was just raccoons' way of eating and not a way to clean food.

It's possible that raccoons like wet food because they often eat from shallow water. It's also possible that raccoons simply like the feeling of rolling food between their paws. However, the dipping motion might just be a habit raccoons are born with.

Eating Everything!

Raccoons are **omnivores**, which means they eat both plants and animals. Sweet corn is a special treat for raccoons. But they'll eat whatever they find: seeds, berries, mice, insects, crayfish, and frogs, as well as pet food on your porch or food in your garbage can.

Chapter 4
Survivors!

A raccoon's sharp claws help it climb up and down trees and hold on to branches. The claws also help a raccoon tear into anything!

No Fuss

Raccoons eat almost anything, including food that was left behind by people or other animals. Not being fussy eaters helps raccoons survive. They can live in many different **habitats** and eat whatever they find there.

Raccoons don't build homes. They move into places other animals have moved out of. Raccoons change homes about every other day. Although their favorite home is a hollow high in a tree, raccoons will live inside a log on the ground, in a chimney, or even in your attic!

Changing to Survive

Raccoons were living in the Americas long before European explorers and settlers arrived. Since that time, trees have been cut down, towns and cities have appeared, and the land has been changed forever. All these changes robbed many animals of their natural homes and sources of food.

But not raccoons! Raccoons changed their ways to fit their changing habitat. They learned to live around people.

Safe Drops

Raccoons have a lot of padding to survive falls. A 40-foot (12-m) drop from a tall tree won't hurt most raccoons.

33

Growing Up

When a female raccoon is ready to give birth in the spring, she looks for a den high in a tree where her young kits will be safe from predators. Newborn kits can't open their eyes until they're about 3 weeks old. A mother raccoon has to move the kits when she goes to search for food or a new den. She uses her mouth to carry them gently, one by one, by the back of the neck. The kits must stay close to their mother to keep warm and to drink her milk.

After about 2 months, the kits are ready to take a look at the world outside the den. They can walk and climb. Each one weighs about 2 pounds (0.9 kg). They follow their mother wherever she goes and do exactly what she does.

The kits spend the summer and fall learning everything they can from their mother. When they're 5 months old, they'll know how to find food on their own. But the kits will stay close to their mother and to each other for the next few months. They'll be able to live on their own when they're about 10 months old.

Kit Stuff

Most female raccoons have three or four kits at a time. A kit is born with short, gray fuzz all over its body. Its dark eye mask grows in by the time it's 10 days old. Its fur coat also grows in over time.

Tiny Tot

A newborn kit is so small it could fit into the palm of your hand!

A baby raccoon learns how to find food in shallow water by watching how its mother uses her paws to catch food and bring it to her mouth. Then the kit does the same.

Staying Alive

Raccoons don't have many predators. Cougars, jaguars, coyotes, foxes, and owls are among the animals that threaten raccoons in the wild. In cities and suburbs, humans are the main danger. Many raccoons are killed by cars. In some places, hunters kill raccoons for food and fur.

Raccoons cause problems for many farmers because they eat crops. Some farmers train dogs to hunt raccoons. Raccoons bring trouble to other people by ruining gardens, knocking over garbage cans, and hiding in garages and houses.

Wild and Free

Some people think raccoons are so cute that they would make good pets. Wildlife experts say absolutely not. Raccoons can carry **rabies** and other harmful diseases. Most important, raccoons are wild animals, and they should live in their natural habitats.

The National Mammal

Some people think the raccoon should be the national mammal, just as the bald eagle is our national bird. They say raccoons deserve this honor because they're brave, clever, adaptable, and tough.

Chapter 5
Raccoons in the World

Where Raccoons Live

Canada

United States

NORTH AMERICA

Mexico

Belize
Honduras
Guatemala
Nicaragua
El Salvador
Panama
Costa Rica

Guyana
Surinam

CENTRAL AMERICA

Venezuela
French Guiana

Colombia

Ecuador

Peru

Brazil

Bolivia

SOUTH AMERICA

Paraguay

Chile

Argentina

Uruguay

The **orange** area shows where raccoons live.

Raccoon Homes

Raccoons live in most parts of North America, Central America, and South America. The only areas where they're not found are middle and northern Canada, the Rocky Mountain region, and the southern part of South America. They're able to survive in very different habitats—from forests to deserts (as long as there's water).

Raccoons usually live near water and near trees that shed leaves. But they also live on prairies and farmland. Raccoons make their homes in trees, logs, and underground holes.

Some raccoons have moved from their natural habitats in the wild to cities and suburbs. Raccoons make their homes in garages, chimneys, sheds, drain pipes, and anywhere else they can create a den.

About 60 years ago, some people took raccoons to Europe and Asia to raise them for their fur and to live in zoos. Over time, some of the raccoons escaped and started families of their own. Now there are very small groups of raccoons in these parts of the world, too.

Raccoon Relatives

Raccoons have a few cousins that look a lot like them. One is the coati (koh-AH-tee). It has a striped tail and markings on its face. But the coati's body, tail, and snout are longer than the raccoon's. Unlike raccoons, coatis are active during the day and often travel in large groups.

Another raccoon look-alike is the ringtail. It's grayish tan and has a white ring around each eye. Its big, bushy tail is much longer than its body, with up to 18 black-and-white rings. Ringtails live in North America, mostly in dry, rocky places.

Some scientists think raccoons are related to a big animal that lives in Asia. It's black and white and has black fur around each eye. If you've guessed that it's the giant panda, you're right!

Fast Facts About Raccoons

Scientific name	*Procyon lotor*
Class	Mammalia
Order	Carnivora
Size	20 to 40 inches (50 to 100 cm) long, including the tail
Weight	5 to 30 pounds (2.3 to 13.6 kg)
Life span	5 years in the wild Up to 20 years in **captivity**
Habitat	Wooded areas with rivers and lakes; cities; suburbs

Coatis live in northern South America, Central America, Mexico, and the southwestern United States.

Glossary

captivity—the state of being caged

guard hairs—long, rough hairs that form the outer layer of fur

habitat—the natural environment where an animal or plant lives

hibernate—to be in a sleeplike state for an extended period of time, usually during winter

instinct—an inborn behavior

nocturnal—active at night

omnivore—an animal that eats both meat and plants

Smart Stuff!

The way raccoons use their paws shows how clever they are. Some people say they're almost as smart as chimpanzees. Raccoons have excellent memories, too. They can learn things after just one experience.

pupil—the black part in the center of an eye that lets in light

predator—an animal that hunts and eats other animals to survive

rabies—a deadly disease that affects the central nervous system of warm-blooded animals

retina—the layers that line the inside of the eye. It receives images formed by the lens and sends them to the brain.

snout—a part of an animal's head that sticks out and is made up of the nose and mouth

Raccoons: Show What You Know

How much have you learned about raccoons? Grab a piece of paper and a pencil and write your answers down.

1. "Raccoon" comes from a Native American word meaning what?

2. How often do raccoons make new dens?

3. How many teeth does a raccoon have?

4. What are guard hairs?

5. What does "nocturnal" mean?

6. What does *lotor* in the raccoon's scientific name, *Procyon lotor*, mean?

7. How do kits learn to find food for themselves?

8. About how many kits does a mother raccoon have at one time?

9. In which areas of the world do most raccoons live?

10. About how long do raccoons live in the wild?

1. "He who scratches with his hands" 2. About every other night 3. Forty 4. Hairs that make up the outer layer of raccoon's fur and act as a raincoat 5. Active at night rather than during day 6. "Washing" 7. By watching their mother 8. Three or four 9. North America, Central America, and South America 10. 5 years

For More Information

Books

Crossingham, John, and Bobbie Kalman. *The Life Cycle of a Raccoon.*
New York, NY: Crabtree Publishing Company, 2003.

Hancock, Lynn. *Tabasco the Saucy Raccoon.* Winlaw, BC, Canada:
Sono Nis Press, 2006.

Landau, Elaine. *Raccoons: Scavengers of the Night.* Berkeley Heights, NJ:
Enslow Publishers, 2008.

Web Sites

Procyon lotor
animaldiversity.ummz.umich.edu/site/accounts/information/Procyon_lotor.html
Read extensive information about raccoons and enjoy dozens of photos of
raccoons in their natural habitats.

Raccoons
www.hsus.org/wildlife/a_closer_look_at_wildlife/raccoons.html
Read interesting facts about raccoons from the Humane Society of the United
States. Find links to many other common animals.

Publisher's note to educators and parents: Our editors have carefully reviewed these Web sites
to ensure that they are suitable for students. Many Web sites change frequently, however, and we
cannot guarantee that a site's future contents will continue to meet our high standards of quality and
educational value. Be advised that students should be closely supervised whenever they access the Internet.

Index